MODERN ERAS UNCOVERED

the early 1900s to 1919

From the Wright Brothers to the Treaty of Versailles

Sean Sheehan

www.raintreepublishers.co.uk
Visit our website to find out more information about **Raintree** books.

To order:
☎ Phone 44 (0) 1865 888113
📄 Send a fax to 44 (0) 1865 314091
💻 Visit the Raintree Bookshop at **www.raintreepublishers.co.uk** to browse our catalogue and order online.

First published in Great Britain by Raintree, Halley Court, Jordan Hill, Oxford, OX2 8EJ, part of Harcourt Education.
Raintree is a registered trademark of Harcourt Education Ltd.

Editorial: Melanie Copland, Tameika Martin, and Lucy Beevor
Design: Michelle Lisseter and Bridge Creatives Services Ltd
Picture Research: Mica Brancic and Ginny Stroud-Lewis
Production: Duncan Gilbert

Originated by Chroma Graphics (Overseas) Pte. Ltd
Printed and bound in China by South China Printing Company

ISBN 1 844 43950 X (hardback)
10 09 08 07 06
10 9 8 7 6 5 4 3 2 1

British Library Cataloguing in Publication Data
Sheehan, Sean
From the Wright Brothers to the Treaty of Versailles. – (Modern Eras Uncovered)
909.8'21
A full catalogue record for this book is available from the British Library.

Acknowledgements
Alamy/V&A Images p. 17; Corbis p. 7; Corbis/Bettmann pp. 4, 15, 27, 31, 33, 36–37, 45; Corbis/Stefano Bianchetti p. 16 (bottom); Corbis/The Hulton Deutsche Collection p. 49; Corbis/Underwood & Underwood pp. 9, 22; Getty Images p. 29; Getty Images/Hulton Archive pp. 26, 28, 30, 32, 35, 39, 41, 42, 43; Getty Images/Hulton Archive/Topical Press Agency p. 8; Getty Images/Time Life Pictures p. 12, 23; Getty Images/Time Life Pictures © Succession Picasso/DACS 2004 p. 19; The Bridgeman Art Library/ © Succession H Matisse/DACS 2004 p. 18; Hulton Archive p. 21; Mary Evans Picture Library p. 10; Mary Evans Picture Library/Sigmund Freud Copyrights p. 14; The Art Archive, Private Collection/Dagli Orti © DACS 2004 p. 46; The Advertising Archives Ltd p. 13; The Art Archive/Dagli Orti p. 16 (top), 24; The Bridgeman Art Library/ © DACS 2004 p. 47; The Art Archive/The Imperial War Museum, London p. 34.

Cover photograph (top) reproduced with permission of Getty Images/AFP, Library of Congress, and photograph (bottom) reproduced with permission of Mary Evans Picture Library.

CONTENTS

Any words appearing in the text in bold, **like this**, are explained in the glossary.

A DIFFERENT KIND OF WORLD

On 1 January 1900, people celebrated the beginning of a new century. Unlike 1 January 2000, there were no televisions showing pictures of New Year's Day festivities around the world. Television had not yet been invented. There were no radios or computers in people's homes, or aeroplanes in the sky. Cars and cinemas were very new inventions that only some people might have heard about. Most people around the world were still living and working in the countryside and growing much of their own food. Many cities, though, such as New York, United States, were beginning to grow larger as people moved there from the countryside.

For reasons like these, the world of 1900 was very different from the one we are now living in. Yet by 1918, when the First World War came to an end, the world had already become a very different place for people in many countries. They were living in a century that would see more changes than any other century in human history.

In the early 1900s, overcrowding of cities meant many people lived in slums, such as these in New York.

Old empires, new ideas

An **empire** is a group of countries (called **colonies**) that are controlled by another country. At the start of the 20th century, the United States was starting to create an empire, as other countries had. China, Turkey, and Russia had ruled over many other countries that were part of their empires for hundreds of years. European countries, especially the UK and France, were building-up empires. In 1900 the UK had the largest empire, covering a quarter of the world and including over 350 million people.

Racism

The words "racism" and "racist" were not around in 1900. This was mostly because white people in Europe and North America at that time had been brought up to believe that they were superior to all non-white people. It was not considered wrong to treat people of other races unfairly or badly. These attitudes were perfectly normal for most white people, so there was no need for a word to describe them.

By 1919 world events had changed many people's views of life. There were new and **radical** ideas in science and **culture**, and a different kind of world was starting to take shape. People in colonies were growing restless under the foreign governments that ruled their countries. In many countries, poor and underpaid people were becoming angry at the way they were controlled by a small number of rich and powerful people. Many of these changing views were caused by the experiences people had during the First World War from 1914 to 1918.

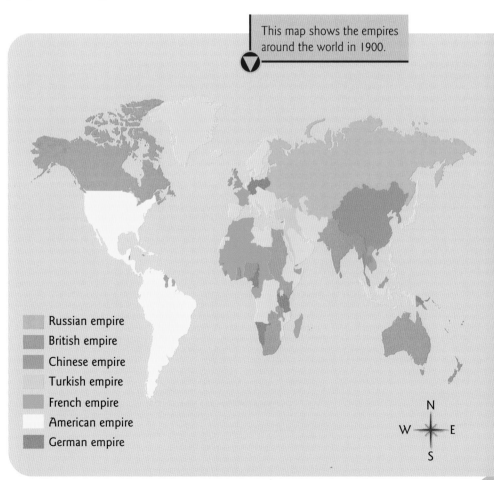

This map shows the empires around the world in 1900.

Russian empire
British empire
Chinese empire
Turkish empire
French empire
American empire
German empire

N
W — E
S

In 1901, rather than 1900, Britain officially celebrated the beginning of a new century. The people of Britain looked to the future with confidence. The future, however, was not to be so rosy. As if to signal the end of an **era**, Queen Victoria died before the end of January 1901. She had been queen for over 63 years, and her name marked a period of history when Britain had ruled the world. The Victorian age was now over.

Birth of the American century

In 1901, President McKinley of the United States was **assassinated** and Theodore Roosevelt, known as "Teddy", became the next president. Roosevelt's presidency was the start of what would eventually become known as the American century.

Europe had been the centre of international power for around four hundred years. In the early 20th century, however, the United States gradually started to replace Britain as a world **economic** power. The United States was rich in natural resources such as oil and coal. The population had lots of energy and talent, enriched by a continuous flow of **immigrants** from Europe. This provided the basis for rapid development, and the wealth and power that was created allowed the United States to begin setting up its own empire.

United States territories overseas

The United States had won a war against Spain in 1898 and had claimed Puerto Rico, Cuba, Guam, and the Philippines from Spanish control. In 1901, a **rebellion** in the Philippines was crushed by US troops. In the same year, Roosevelt announced that the United States had the right to protect its **territories** in the Caribbean. When Cuba became a **republic**, free from United States control in 1902, and US troops left the island, Roosevelt insisted on setting up a naval base at Guantánamo Bay in the south of Cuba.

The United States also got involved with Panama in 1903, so that Panama could grant them the right to build and operate the Panama Canal. Further involvement by the United States occurred in the Dominican Republic in 1904 and in Nicaragua in 1912. Hawaii was taken over to stop Japan from getting there first, and in 1917 the United States bought the Virgin Islands from Denmark for US$25 million.

Teddy bears

Toy stuffed bears were not called teddy bears until Theodore Roosevelt went on a bear hunt in 1902. A bear cub was caught and tied to a tree, but the president refused to shoot the helpless creature. The story appeared in a newspaper with a cartoon. The cartoonist continued to use the bear whenever the president was in the news and the animal turned into a cuddly creature with large ears. A New York shop selling home-made stuffed bears began labelling them "Teddy's Bear" and the idea caught on. In 1907, one manufacturer sold nearly a million teddy bears and this new term entered the English language.

This huge shipping lock on the Panama Canal was built in April 1913.

Discontent in the cities

The economic power of countries like Germany, the UK, and the United States depended on large-scale industries, such as steel production and shipbuilding. By 1900, all three countries had several large cities where wages were low, workers were crowded into poor areas, and life was hard. In 1900, Britain raised the starting age for coal miners from twelve to thirteen. People who were ill or unemployed had no money to live on at all. Only Germany had a basic system of **social security**, where the government gave some groups of people a bit of money to live on.

Working people had, however, organized themselves into groups called **trade unions**. By acting together, workers in a trade union hoped to improve their working conditions and wages. In 1905, the Industrial Workers of the World organization was formed in the United States to improve the lives of workers. In Britain five years earlier, trade unions had helped to form the Labour Party. They hoped to have their own representatives elected to **parliament**.

Some trade unions organized **strikes** – where workers refused to work until improvements were made to their rates of pay or conditions of work. Some employers used private police forces, and governments used their armies, to oppose striking workers. In 1906, the French army crushed a wave of strikes that broke out across the country. In 1909, in Barcelona, Spain, troops were ordered to open fire on strikers but refused and joined them instead! In 1911, two striking dock workers were shot dead by troops in Liverpool.

Liverpool dock workers meet during the dock strike of 1911.

Votes for women

In 1902, Australia followed New Zealand and became the second country in the world to give women the right to vote in national elections. In other countries, women had to struggle hard to get the vote. In Britain, the women who gained the most publicity when calling for the right to vote became known as **suffragettes**. They chained themselves to public buildings, threw bricks through shop windows, and worked hard to draw attention to their cause. When they were arrested and imprisoned they went on **hunger strike**. In 1913, the suffragette Emily Wilding Davison died after grabbing the reins of a horse and being trampled on at the British Derby horse race as an act of protest.

Some western states in the United States gave women the vote in the early years of the new century, but it was 1920 before all women in the United States had the right to vote. In the UK all women were given the vote in 1928.

△ Three police officers arrest a suffragette outside Buckingham Palace, London, June 1914.

Strikes and violence

In the United States the worst cases of violence used against strikers were carried out by company guards or private detective agencies. It was not unusual for a company to employ the services of armed guards who worked for a detective agency. Their job would be to try to force strikers to return to work. Sometimes this resulted in acts of violence and even murder. The Baldwin Felts Detective Agency, in Colorado, even had its own armoured car fitted with a machine gun.

First wars of the century

A war was already in progress on New Year's Day in southern Africa. It had started there in 1899, between the Boers and the British. The Boers were descendants of Europeans who had settled in two Dutch colonies in southern Africa. When large deposits of gold were found in Boer territory, the British wanted to establish their own rule there. The Boers were determined to stay independent of British rule and a war developed between the two sides.

The Boer War

The British army had much better military forces, but the Boers, who were mostly farmers, used **guerrilla** methods of fighting. They proved very difficult to defeat. The British, humiliated by not achieving a quick victory, began using new tactics to defeat the determined farmers who were fighting to protect their way of life. The British divided up the countryside, burnt the farms of the Boers, and gathered the women and children into special areas that they were not allowed to leave. In doing this, the British created the world's first **concentration camps**. The dreadful conditions in the camps led to the deaths of over 25,000 Boers. In other concentration camps, created for black people who worked for the Boers, around 20,000 people died.

The war dragged on until the farmers surrendered in 1902. They were promised the right to carry on with their traditional way of life, which included treating the native black population as an **inferior** race.

Boer prisoners are escorted into a prison by armed guards in 1900.

Russian-Japanese war

The leaders of Japan wanted to copy the success of European countries and build-up their own empire by gaining control of Manchuria, in northern China, and Korea. Russia, who also wanted this territory for its own empire, was determined to stop this happening. Japan decided to gain the advantage over Russia and launched a surprise attack in 1904. They attacked Port Arthur on the Chinese coast, where the Russians had a naval base. The Russian fleet was **blockaded** and their army defeated in various battles. This was the first time in modern history that an Asian army had defeated a European one. When the war ended in 1905, other countries realized that Japanese power was growing.

This map shows the borders of eastern Russia, Japan, and Manchuria in China in 1905.

Russia

Manchuria

China

Korea

Japan

Death in the camps

In 1901, a British woman named Emily Hobhouse wrote what she saw when she visited a concentration camp for Boers:

"A girl of twenty-one lay dying on a stretcher. Her father, a big, gentle Boer, was kneeling beside her. In the next tent, his wife was watching a child of six, also dying. I can't describe what it is like to see these children lying about in a state of collapse. It's just exactly like faded flowers thrown away. And one has to stand and look on at such misery and be able to do almost nothing."

(FROM *THE MAMMOTH BOOK OF HOW IT HAPPENED* EDITED BY JON E. LEWIS)

Inventions and discoveries

Orville Wright takes to the air in *Flyer* as his brother Wilbur looks on at Kitty Hawk, 1903.

In 1900, there were no aeroplanes in the sky. The closest humans had got to flying was in an airship in France in 1852, but this was more like a hot-air balloon. Powered aircraft had not yet been invented.

At the beginning of the 20th century Orville and Wilbur Wright, two brothers from Dayton, Ohio, in the United States, were experimenting with gliders and lightweight aeroplane engines. In 1903, at Kitty Hawk, North Carolina, the first successful flight of a powered aircraft took place when their *Flyer* machine took off and stayed in the air for 12 seconds. In time to come, this event would be compared with the moon landings as one of the great moments in history. The age of flight had begun.

There were many other developments in science and technology at this time. In 1901, an Italian engineer, Guglielmo Marconi, made the first wireless **transmission** across the Atlantic Ocean using radio waves. In 1905, fingerprints were now being used widely to convict criminals.

Up, Up, and Away

In December 1903, Orville Wright sent a telegram to his father after their plane made four successful flights:

SUCCESS. FOUR FLIGHTS, THURSDAY MORNING, ALL AGAINST A TWENTY-ONE MILE WIND. STARTED FROM LEVEL GROUND, WITH ENGINE POWER ALONE. AVERAGE SPEED THROUGH AIR THIRTY-ONE MILES. INFORM PRESS. HOME AT CHRISTMAS.

(FROM *MIRACLE AT KITTY HAWK* BY FRED C. KELLY)

Improving life

Millions of ordinary people experienced the power of electricity for the first time when street lamps began operating in parts of London in the 1900s. In the cities of the United States, one in ten homes had some form of electric power by 1900, but the new technology was still only available to the rich. This was also true when the world's first automatic telephone exchange started working in Massachusetts in 1900. It carried 10,000 lines that could work up to a distance of just 1 mile (1.6 kilometres).

An invention that reached ordinary people more quickly than electricity or the telephone was a new type of shaving razor with a double-edged blade, invented by King C. Gillette from Chicago, United States. The fact that old blades could be thrown away and the Gillette razor fitted with a new one was important to its success. It meant people could shave with sharp blades all of the time, for much less money. It first went on sale in 1903 and by the end of the following year around 90,000 razors and 12,400,000 blades had been sold. Older razors were called cut-throat razors because the whole of the blade was dangerously exposed. The Gillette razor became known as the "safety razor" because it meant men could shave safely with only the thin edge of the blade exposed.

A British engineer called Hubert Booth invented the first vacuum cleaner in 1901. Powered by a petrol engine, its four long suction hoses were transported in a horse-drawn cart, which would pull up outside a house. The hoses, stretching up to 30 metres (100 feet) in length, were passed through windows and into rooms that needed to be vacuumed. Only the rich could afford this service. William Hoover, from Ohio, United States, developed the first portable electric vacuum cleaner in 1908.

This is one of the first adverts for an early vacuum cleaner, on sale in the UK in the 1900s.

13

NEW WAYS OF SEEING THE WORLD

Britain's Industrial Revolution began towards the end of the 18th century. By the beginning of the 20th century it had changed the way of life for everyone. The world became a different place. There were new machines, new ways of travelling, and new classes of people. Nothing seemed beyond the scope of engineers and scientists, and artists also began to question the traditional ways of representing the world.

Surprises and secrets

In 1895, a scientist called Ernest Rutherford travelled from New Zealand to Cambridge University in the UK. He made important new discoveries in the field of science. His experiments showed how **electrons** travelled around the centre of an **atom**, in a similar way to the planets going around the Sun. He worked with other scientists who later went on to develop the first **atomic bombs**.

Freud and dreams

In 1900, Sigmund Freud, an Austrian doctor, had a book published called *The Interpretation of Dreams*. Freud showed how people's behaviour can be affected by feelings that we do not always want to admit to ourselves – this was a very new way of explaining behaviour! Freud said that as well as the **conscious** mind, there is also an **unconscious** mind, and that our dreams can give clues about what our unconscious mind is trying to hide. Different groups of people, from artists to psychologists, began to be influenced by the new ideas of Freud.

This drawing shows Sigmund Freud at work at his desk.

In 1905, a young German, Albert Einstein, published some ideas about time and space that shocked scientists around the world. He argued, and was later proved to be right, that completely new laws of science were needed. Einstein's ideas were totally radical – nothing like them had ever been heard before – and they changed the field of science called physics forever. His ideas became the starting point for many more developments in science.

Einstein demonstrates mathematical formulas to a meeting of Californian scientists in January 1931.

Albert Einstein

Einstein, born in Germany in 1879, was encouraged by his parents to be independent. He was expelled from school, although he was thinking of leaving anyway, and moved with his parents to Italy when he was fifteen. He went to university in Switzerland and began writing scientific papers. Einstein was Jewish but he was not a religious person. He was against war and was attracted to **socialism**.

Einstein experienced **discrimination** because he was Jewish, and he was later forced to leave Germany because of this. Before his scientific theories were proved correct, he said that if he was proved right the Germans would call him a German, but that if he was proved wrong they would call him a Jew.

New art and design

Art nouveau, French for 'new art', developed in the final decades of the 19th century and by 1900 it had spread across Europe and the United States. Art nouveau followers said the art that came before it was too concerned with just copying traditional ideas. A new generation of artists, designers, and architects were determined to create a new art form for the modern age in which they lived. Large industrial cities, such as Paris, Berlin, Barcelona, Glasgow, Vienna, New York, and Chicago, all developed their own forms of art and design that became recognizable as art nouveau.

This art nouveau-inspired desk was created by the French designer Eugene Vallin.

Art for cities

Art nouveau was a reaction to **industrialization** and city life, and artists and designers responded to this new world in different ways. Many wanted to create a sense of beauty by using their artistic skills to create interesting everyday objects. Posters advertising cigarettes, glass perfume bottles, signs for underground train stations, restaurant displays, lampshades – things as varied and ordinary as these became known as forms of art nouveau.

Designers and artists were excited by the new materials they could work with. Some worked with cast iron, others specialized in poster art. Hector Guimard in France became famous for his designs for the new Paris underground system, the Métro, which began construction in 1900.

The swirling patterns on the new Paris underground became well-known across the world.

Beautiful forms

While art nouveau celebrated city life, it also realized that there were ugly aspects to it. Some art nouveau artists wanted to turn away from this towards a fantasy world. They used long, swirling lines in their art that looked wild and natural, and they often used the shapes of animals such as peacocks, and plants such as orchids in their work. Winding, snake-like lines were also popular in art nouveau designs.

This silk furnishing fabric, designed by Robert Bonfils in France, shows how nature was used in art nouveau design.

Interior design

Art nouveau also changed the way architects designed buildings and the way people decorated their homes. One of the most important architects of the new century was the American Frank Lloyd Wright. He insisted that the inside and outside of a building should be designed together and kept simple so as to bring out the natural qualities of the materials being used. Designers began enlarging the size of windows and adding colour using stained-glass panels.

An ordinary perfume bottle is transformed into a beautiful object by the designer Hector Guimard.

Wild beasts and Picasso

For most of the 19th century, artists painted pictures of everyday objects and scenes. The traditional view was that art was like a mirror, reflecting the world as we normally see it. Paintings were praised if, like photographs, they looked just like real life. All this changed in the early years of the 20th century. The "mirror" was broken and painters began to experiment and paint in completely new ways.

Wild beasts

The city of Paris acted like a magnet for painters who had turned their backs on traditional forms of art. In 1905, when some of their paintings were exhibited in a show, a critic described them as *fauves* (French for "wild beasts") and their style of painting became known as fauvism.

Henri Matisse was seen as the leader of the "wild beasts" and many people thought his work was scandalous. Critics who could not understand his way of painting rubbished *The Green Stripe* – a portrait of Matisse's wife, with a bright green streak down her face. Matisse made his paintings vibrant and used colours in a new way – not to capture a scene like a photograph, but to show feelings.

▲ *The Dance* (1909) is another painting by Henri Matisse that shows bright colours and vivid movement.

Inspired by Africa

Parts of Africa were French colonies, and stolen African art, especially sculptures and small statues, began appearing in Paris. When Matisse showed this art to a young Spanish painter, Pablo Picasso, the result was a new kind of painting. Inspired by African art, Picasso painted *Les Demoiselles D'Avignon* ("Young Women of Avignon"), a portrait of five women that shocked people. The women looked powerful, but not glamorous, with twisted bodies and mask-like heads.

Cubism

Georges Braque was another French painter who was very impressed by Picasso's work. The two men became friends and worked together. Their style of painting became known as Cubism because, according to a critic, everything was painted in "little cubes". In cubist art, different points of view were presented in the same painting and this was a very original idea. In 1913, the new art from Europe was exhibited at the Armory exhibition in New York, United States. This was the city's most important art exhibition at that time. From then on, the new ideas in European art began to influence the work of American artists.

Picasso's *Les Demoiselles D'Avignon* shocked people who were used to the "traditional" painting style of the 19th century.

Pablo Picasso

Picasso was only eighteen when he boarded a train in Barcelona, Spain for Paris, France in 1900. At school in Spain he had been a rebel, but his talent as a painter was quickly recognized. Even though he could not speak French, he went to Paris because he knew that was where new artists were working and where art from Africa was being displayed. African art, he said, was "against everything, against unknown, threatening spirits. I too am against everything. I too believe that everything is unknown."

EMPIRES AROUND THE WORLD

In the early part of the 20th century people in Britain relied mainly on newspapers to tell them what was happening in other parts of the world. Wealthy people read *The Times* newspaper, while new newspapers such as the *Daily Mail* and the *Daily Express* were reaching a larger audience of readers. Foreign news was usually kept short and was often exaggerated. Most people had no way of checking the truth of foreign news and a newspaper would sometimes alter the truth or even make up a story if it would help to sell the paper.

Australia

At the start of the century, Australia was made up of six separate colonies ruled by Britain. In 1901, these six colonies joined together and formed the Commonwealth of Australia. The new country was given Dominion status, which meant that Australia could largely govern itself. Most other parts of the British Empire were ruled directly by Britain. In colonies given Dominion status, most of the population were white people. The new nation of Australia was determined to keep it this way and restricted the entry of non-white immigrants.

An economic empire

The growth of the United States empire was less obvious than those of the European nations like Britain and France. It developed through United States companies investing in Central and South America, where they became large landowners. The United States began to get more involved in the actual running of these countries after President Roosevelt's announcement in 1905 that the United States would act as a "policeman" in the Caribbean. In that year, the United States took economic control of the Dominican Republic and in 1912 this happened in Nicaragua as well. This time, US soldiers were also sent because some Nicaraguans were against United States involvement.

Death in the Congo

King Leopold II of Belgium wanted his own empire. He had seen Britain, France, and Germany creating colonies in Africa and grabbed an unclaimed part for himself. Africans in the Congo lived in simple mud huts and had their own system of tribal rules. But by 1900, King Leopold had owned the Congo for fifteen years and had become extremely rich by selling ivory and rubber abroad. This wealth, however, was made at the expense of thousands of Africans who were forced to work as slaves.

This village tribal scene is from the Belgian Congo (now known as the Democratic Republic of Congo) in 1900. Africans such as these were forced to work as slaves by many colonial rulers.

"You are only beasts yourselves"

Roger Casement was working for the British government in Africa in the 1900s. He reported what was happening in the Congo in 1903. He included this account by an African worker:

"We had to go further and further into the forest to find the rubber vines. Then we became starving. We begged the white men to leave us alone, saying we could get no more rubber, but the white men and their soldiers said: 'Go! You are only beasts yourselves.'"

(FROM *PORTRAIT OF A DECADE* BY TREVOR FISHER)

Resistance and rebellion

The people in countries that were ruled by empires did not always accept their position. Rebellions and uprisings broke out in a number of places, but governments used their armies to put down acts of resistance.

Genocide in Africa

Hereroland in southern Africa, which is now part of the country of Namibia, became a German colony in 1884. The Herero people began losing their land to white settlers. In 1904, angry with what was happening to them, they armed themselves and refused to obey the Germans. The Germans crushed this uprising. Afterwards, the German Commander General von Trotha decided to kill all the Herero people.

General von Trotha had his soldiers gather the Herero and force them into the desert. Soldiers were ordered to shoot any Herero who tried to return. Around 60,000 Hereros were killed over the next two years.

The Boxer Rebellion

By the end of the 19th century many Chinese people were angry because European countries, the United States, and Japan had set themselves up in Chinese ports. They were setting up businesses as if the ports belonged to them. The Boxer rebellion broke out against this in 1900. It took its name from a Chinese group who practised boxing in the hope it would make them strong against attack. Foreigners in China were attacked and killed. The rebels seized Peking (Beijing) and took control of the European quarter of the city. After 55 days, the Boxer rebels were attacked by a European and American army. During the siege of Peking, the Boxers killed 76 soldiers and 6 children. As an act of revenge, however, thousands of Chinese were murdered.

French soldiers fire at rebels during the Boxer Rebellion of 1900.

Uprising in Petrograd

Russian people were becoming increasingly unhappy with the rule of their own emperor, Tsar Nicholas, because of their poverty and lack of rights. In January 1905, demonstrators gathered outside the palace in Petrograd, thinking the Tsar would help them. Instead, the army fired upon them and hundreds were killed. Protest strikes broke out across Russia and sailors **mutinied** on board the battleship *Potemkin*. In October, the Tsar agreed to the demands for a parliament; the people seemed to have won a great victory. Some Russians, however, thought it was a trick and they set about planning a **revolution** that would remove tsars from power completely.

"A scrap of paper"

Leon Trotsky was one of the Russians who did not believe in the promises made by the Tsar. He made a speech to groups of workers in October 1905:

"Do not celebrate victory yet; it is not yet complete. The Tsar's promise is only a scrap of paper! Today it will be given to us and tomorrow it will be taken away and torn into pieces as I am now tearing it into pieces."

Trotsky stirs up the Red Army troops and the Russian workers during a speech in 1905.

Background to the First World War

The old Turkish empire, known as the Ottoman Empire, was falling apart by the beginning of the 20th century. Its hold over the south-east of Europe, known as the Balkans, had been broken and many countries there were independent by 1900. Turkish influence was weakened more in 1912–1913 when Ottoman forces were attacked and defeated in Serbia, Montenegro, Bulgaria, and Greece.

A threat to peace

Now that Turkey had lost power in the Balkans, other countries were taking an interest in the area. Would the two neighbouring empires (the Austro-Hungarian empire and the Russian empire) fight each other to take control?

In 1908, Bosnia, which was populated by a race of people called Slavs, was seized by Austria-Hungary. There were Slavs in the Austro-Hungarian empire, too, and the empire was afraid that Slavs might join together and threaten its power. Serbia was seen as a huge threat, as it also had a large Slav population and it had already gained independence from Turkey. Austria-Hungary was also afraid that Russia, with its own Slav population, would try to gain influence in the Balkans.

Ottoman soldiers struggle against attacking forces in Serbia in 1912, where they were eventually defeated.

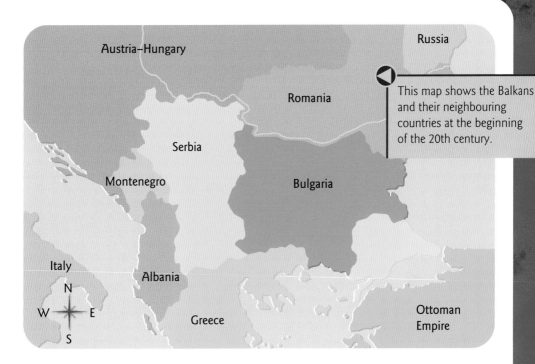

Austria–Hungary

Russia

Romania

Serbia

Montenegro

Bulgaria

Italy

Albania

N

W — E

S

Greece

Ottoman
Empire

This map shows the Balkans
and their neighbouring
countries at the beginning
of the 20th century.

Empires collide

Austria-Hungary was becoming involved
in the Balkans and viewing Russia with
suspicion. Germany also became
involved, because Germany and Austria-
Hungary had been **allies** for a long time.
They had common interests and would
support each other in a war.

Germany was also keen to extend the
size of its empire and catch up with
Britain. Germany began to build up its
navy after Britain started increasing the
size of its navy. The situation in the
Balkans encouraged an **arms race**. As
Germany and Austria-Hungary built up
their armies, so too did Russia.

France became an ally of Russia, so if
Russia went to war against Austria-
Hungary then France was likely to
support Russia. Europe had become an
explosive mix of countries taking sides.

A new president

US presidential elections in 1912 saw the
election of Woodrow Wilson. In the lead
up to the First World War in Europe, in
1914, the United States was more
concerned with events in Mexico where
a civil war had broken out. Wilson sent
troops into Mexico in 1916 to capture
Pancho Villa, who was leading a rebellion
against the Mexican government.

Woodrow Wilson

Woodrow Wilson was the first
Democrat to become president in
the 20th century. His style was very
different from Roosevelt's. He spoke
of the need for governments to have
moral principles. By this he meant
that governments should do what
was right and not just what was in
their own interests. Under Wilson,
the United States entered the First
World War in 1917.

At the start of the 20th century football was becoming a very popular sport for ordinary people in Britain. In 1901, over 100,000 spectators watched the Football Association (FA) Cup Final at Crystal Palace in London. The new Liberal government of 1905 introduced an old age **pension** and the beginnings of a national insurance and unemployment scheme. The Liberals wanted to gain the support of working people and to stop the Labour Party from gaining political power. Local government was also becoming more important and town councils were in charge of public services like the supply of water and sewage facilities.

Life in the city

In large cities, new ideas and technologies were changing people's lifestyles. In 1905, the first purpose-built cinema was opened to the public in Pittsburgh in the United States. It showed *The Great Train Robbery*, the first film in which the camera moved to follow the action. This is where the term "movie" came from. The film did not have sound and lasted only 12 minutes! There were less than a hundred seats, and as each one cost 5 cents (a nickel) the cinema was called the Nickelodeon. Audiences seeing moving images for the first time were sometimes terrified by what they saw. In *The Great Train Robbery*, some people fainted at a scene where one of the train robbers turned his pistol towards the audience.

This is a scene from *The Great Train Robbery*, the first-ever movie.

Sport

Boxing was an extremely popular sport around the world. The American Jack Johnson became the first black boxing champion in 1908, when he beat the Canadian Tommy Burns in Sydney, Australia. This news did not go down well in the southern states of the United States, where there was a lot of racism. Demonstrations took place in some United States cities when the victory in Sydney was announced.

Women

Generally speaking at this time, men did not think of women as their equals and women's rights were not respected. In the United States, the **anarchist** Emma Goldman campaigned for women to use **birth control** and in 1916 she was imprisoned for handing out leaflets on the subject. Most women were housewives and only a few went out to work.

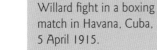

Jack Johnson and Jess Willard fight in a boxing match in Havana, Cuba, 5 April 1915.

Jack Johnson

As a black boxer, and someone who twice married white women, Jack Johnson was the victim of racial prejudice. In 1912, he was sentenced to a year in prison for transporting his wife across US state lines before their marriage. Johnson, disguised as a member of a black baseball team, fled to Canada and was a fugitive for seven years. When he defended his world title against an American white boxer, Jess Willard, in Cuba in 1915, it was thought he deliberately lost the fight in the hope that charges against him would be dropped. This never happened and he surrendered to the authorities and served his prison time in Leavenworth, Kansas.

Disasters

San Francisco earthquake

By 1906 San Francisco was the largest city on the west coast of the United States. Many of its 400,000 people had arrived there as immigrants, or the children of immigrants, or had settled there as **migrants** from eastern states – all in search of a better life. The poor lived in cheaply built, wooden housing blocks that gave no protection against the tremendously powerful earthquake that struck the city at 5:12 a.m. on 18 April 1906.

The earthquake lasted for less than 3 minutes and thousands of buildings fell to the ground. People were buried alive as they lay in their beds. The city had electrified cable cars and an electric lighting system so fires broke out quickly. The fire brigade could not do much to help because the earthquake also broke the main water pipes.

Fires continued to burn for over three days. Around 700 people lost their lives, and two out of every three people found themselves homeless.

Stunned people stand in the rubble of their collapsed houses after the earthquake in San Francisco, 18 April 1906.

"San Francisco is gone!"

The American writer Jack London wrote an account of the San Francisco earthquake:

"San Francisco is gone! Nothing remains of it but memories and some houses on the outskirts. Its industrial area is wiped out. Its social and residential area is wiped out. The factories and warehouses, the great stores and newspaper buildings, the hotels and palaces of the rich – all are gone. In the working-class **ghettos**, and in the factories, fires started. The flames could not be put out. There was no organization, no communication. All the clever developments of a 20th-century city had been smashed by the earthquake."

(FROM "THE SAN FRANCISCO EARTHQUAKE", COLLIER'S WEEKLY, 5 MAY 1906)

The Titanic sinks

The *Titanic*, built in Belfast in the north of Ireland, was celebrated as the most luxurious ocean liner of its time. It sailed from England in 1912 on its maiden voyage to New York, United States, carrying poor immigrants as well as some very rich people. Wealthy passengers, who could afford first class travel, had a part of the ship reserved just for them. Passengers who could only afford third-class tickets had crowded cabins in the lower parts of the ship. On 14 April, 4 days into its voyage, the ship hit an iceberg and sank within 3 hours. The captain gave the order to abandon ship but there were not enough lifeboats to carry everyone to safety. More than 1,500 people died.

First class passengers were the most likely to get a place on a lifeboat, and women and children were offered the first places. The crew of the ship acted bravely and most of them drowned trying to keep the ship afloat long enough to allow passengers to escape. One surviving crew member who saw the ship sinking wrote later: "She was a beautiful sight then. Smoke and sparks were rushing out of her funnel. The ship was turning gradually on her nose – just like a duck that goes for a dive."

The 1997 movie *Titanic* recreated the 1912 disaster using sophisticated special effects.

Mass production

In the 19th century, large factories in Britain were employing hundreds of people to handle machines producing huge amounts of cloth. This is called **mass production**. Most goods, though, were still made by small companies and needed a lot of skill and craftsmanship. By the early years of the 20th century, however, machines were being used for the mass production of all sorts of goods. This was especially the case in the United States.

Workers construct a Model T engine on a Ford Motor Company assembly line in Detroit, United States, 1914.

Ford and the assembly line

It took so long to make the first petrol-driven motor cars that costs were very high and only the very wealthy could afford to buy them. The mass-production of cars began in the United States in 1901. In 1903, Henry Ford set up a car manufacturing company in Detroit. Ford promised to make Detroit "the motor capital of the world" and wanted to make cars more affordable. In 1908, he launched the Model T Ford.

Working-class people could still not afford these cars but some middle-class families were able to buy them. This was especially the case after 1913 when Ford introduced the moving **assembly line** to car factories. Instead of making each car as a whole, a conveyor belt carried the partly-built car from one group of workers to another. Each team had its own machines to complete a particular part of the job. The time taken to produce the body of a Model T Ford was reduced from 12 hours to just over 90 minutes.

To meet the huge demand, Coca Cola™ introduced gas-motored trucks to replace horse-drawn carriages as delivery vehicles, such as this one pictured in 1913.

Bottles and Pyrex™

Developments in the technology of glass making led to factories mass-producing bottles. By 1910, bottles were being churned out at the rate of 2,500 per hour. This was ten times the production rate of the 1890s.

Since 1895 Coca-Cola™ had been available in every part of the United States and demand was growing – so more bottles were needed! In 1900, Coca-Cola™ arrived in Britain for the first time, but it was another fifteen years before the Coca-Cola™ bottle was given its famous shape. In 1915, an American company called Pyrex Corning introduced a new type of glassware. This company was producing glass that would not shatter into pieces when it was heated.

Detroit

Detroit in the United States developed into a major industrial city in the early decades of the 20th century. Other car companies followed Ford to the city and, during the First World War, new factories began producing weapons as well. Detroit became a magnet for people seeking jobs. It also attracted large numbers of black people from the southern states of the United States. As well as finding work, black migrants also hoped to escape racism, which was very strong in the south. They were partly successful in this although, in time, Detroit developed its own racial problems.

THE FIRST WORLD WAR

Many ordinary people in Britain supported the idea of going to war against Germany when the First World War broke out on 4 August 1914. There was a general feeling that the fighting would not last for very long, and people thought: "it will all be over by Christmas". Men rushed to volunteer to fight, and a wave of **patriotism** swept over the country.

British volunteers march alongside armed officers following the outbreak of the First World War in 1914.

The short-term causes of the war

Archduke Franz Ferdinand, **heir** to the Austro-Hungarian throne, and his wife were assassinated in Sarajevo, the capital of Bosnia, in June 1914. The assassins were a group of **nationalists** who wanted Bosnia to be independent from Austria-Hungary. The nationalists were Serbs and Austria-Hungary used the assassination as an excuse to declare war on Serbia. Russia chose to help Serbia and began **mobilizing** its army. The French, allies of Russia, did the same. Germany, an ally of Austria-Hungary, declared war on Russia and France. When German troops crossed into Belgium on their way to France, Britain declared war on Germany. Other countries, such as Italy and Turkey, joined in, choosing to help the side that could offer them the most if it won.

The long-term causes of the war

Each of the powerful European countries had their own reasons for going to war:

- Austria-Hungary wanted to punish the Serbs and stop Serbian nationalism from weakening its empire
- Russia wanted power and influence in the Balkans and it wanted Austria-Hungary to be made weaker
- Germany wanted to increase its power to make it equal with Britain and France – countries with larger empires
- France, an old enemy of Germany, wanted to teach Germany a lesson
- Britain did not want to stand by and see whoever won become **dominant** in Europe. If Germany won, Britain would have felt very threatened by its economic and military power. Britain hoped to defeat Germany and remove this possible threat to its own power.

Serb nationalist, Gavrilo Princip, is led into custody after assassinating Archduke Ferdinand and his wife in Sarajevo, Bosnia, June 1914.

The United States and the war

At the start of the First World War most Americans did not see it as having much to do with them. It was seen as a squabble involving European powers and their empires. When President Woodrow Wilson was campaigning for re-election in 1916 he promised people that the United States would not get involved in the war. He won the election, but the following year his promise was broken and the United States joined the war.

"The Serbs started it"

In 1914, 12-year-old German, Piete Kuhr, wrote in her diary about the start of the First World War:

"The Serbs started it. Austria-Hungary, Germany, Serbia, Russia, and France joined in. We have no idea what war will be like. There are flags on all the houses in town just as if we were having a festival."

(FROM *A WAR IN WORDS* EDITED BY SVETLANA PALMER AND SARAH WALLIS)

The war drags on

People who had believed that the war would be short were wrong. The German army marched through Belgium and northern France, and the Russians marched towards Berlin in Germany. The French joined with the British to fight back against the German invasion. The armies dug in with neither side able to break the **deadlock**. At the same time, further east, Austria-Hungary and Germany pushed back against the Russians.

This painting of a shattered war landscape is called the *Menin Road*. The artist, Paul Nash, was a soldier on the Western Front during the First World War.

Battlefields

In 1915, British troops were joined by troops from Australia and New Zealand as they tried to seize Gallipoli, a **peninsula** in Turkey. They hoped to knock out Turkey, which was an ally of Germany. The troops were killed trying to land on the beaches and those who made it ashore dug into **trenches** until they were finally pulled back.

In February 1916, the Germans attacked the French at Verdun with a massive show of **artillery** power. The French fought back with their own artillery and each side lost over 300,000 men. In July 1916, the British, under the command of Field Marshal Douglas Haig, joined the French in attacking German forces in an area called the Somme in France. The Battle of the Somme, like Verdun, turned into a bloodbath. On the first day of the battle over 60,000 British troops were killed or wounded. By the end of all the battles in this area, close to 1 million British, French, and German soldiers lay dead.

The Zimmermann telegram

Arthur Zimmermann became Germany's foreign affairs secretary in November 1916. In January 1917, he sent a coded telegram to Germany's **ambassador** in Mexico. He suggested that if the United States joined the war then Mexico should fight on Germany's side against the United States. If the United States was then defeated, Texas, New Mexico, and Arizona would be given to Mexico as its reward.

This telegram was decoded by British intelligence and on 1 March 1917 it was published in US newspapers. This helped to change US public opinion in favour of going to war against Germany.

The United States enters the war

In 1915, the passenger ship *Lusitania* was sunk in the Atlantic by a German submarine. Over a thousand people died, including many US citizens. The Germans then stopped operating in the Atlantic for fear of bringing the United States into the war. However, by 1917, Germany was desperate to win the war and began sinking merchant ships in the Atlantic.

Germany had hoped to defeat Britain before United States' support could make any difference. The United States declared war on Germany in April 1917.

By September of 1917 there were 1,200,000 US troops in Europe, under the command of General John J. Persing. They helped Britain, France, and Russia to defeat Germany. The United States also gave large loans to Britain and France, which allowed them to pay for new weapons and other supplies.

Americans are urged to volunteer for the US Army in a recruitment poster from the First World War.

I WANT YOU FOR U.S. ARMY

NEAREST RECRUITING STATION

Millions dead

By 1917, all the early enthusiasm for the war had disappeared. Morale was low and there were mutinies in France and Italy. Some French troops marched through towns "baa-ing" like sheep, to show that they felt like helpless sheep being driven to slaughter. Some British troops in France rebelled against their orders. The leaders of this rebellion were executed and the rebellion was kept secret.

The war ends

A revolution in Russia in 1917 led to the Russians making peace terms with Germany and pulling out of the war early in 1918. In March 1918, Germany planned a final attack. At first this was successful, but by the summer British and French forces had put an end to it. By this time, US troops and money had arrived to provide extra support and the German army was exhausted. Ordinary Germans were losing faith in their leaders and began plotting to overthrow the government. Some soldiers and sailors refused to fight any longer. On 11 November, at 11a.m., Germany agreed to end the war.

The cost of the war

Around 10 million soldiers died fighting in the First World War and 20 million were wounded. Soldiers from all over the world died, including nearly 2 million Germans, 700,000 British, 250,000 Americans, 60,000 Australians, and 18,000 New Zealanders. India, as part of the British Empire, was also involved in the war and 48,000 Indians also died. At least 7 million civilians died – because of disease, starvation, and other war-related causes.

Row upon row of white crosses in the Meuse-Argonne military cemetery near Romagne, France, mark the graves of US soldiers who died in the First World War.

The costs of the war also included the way it affected those who survived. The war left **psychological** scars on wounded and disabled soldiers. A whole generation of people in the countries involved were affected, too. Citizens looked at the war memorials in their villages and towns, and at the huge war cemeteries containing thousands of rows of graves, and asked themselves why this had happened.

No one had expected a war like this. The new technology of the time had transformed the nature of war. Machine guns, tanks, flame-throwers, submarines, poison gas, and high explosives had made it easy to kill huge numbers of people. Civilians suffered in new ways, bombed from the air by airships or starved to death by naval blockades. People talked of it as "the war to end all wars" and no one could ever imagine this sort of thing happening again.

Spanish flu

Spanish flu, caused by a virus that spread quickly from person to person, killed an estimated 30 million people between 1918 and 1919. It is believed to have started in an army camp in Kansas, United States. Soldiers sent to fight in the First World War took it with them to Europe in April 1918. It then spread to nearly every part of the world. More US soldiers died from Spanish flu than from war injuries, and in India around 12 million people are thought to have died from the virus.

RESULTS OF THE WAR

All over Britain, in every city, town, and village, families and widows felt the cost of the war. The soldiers who had died were mostly young married men or bachelors. In some villages every single man of fighting age was dead. Life had changed in other ways, too. Women had been called on to fill the places of men in factories. By 1918, four out of every ten workers in Britain were women, although they were only paid around half of the usual male wage.

Irish nationalism

After the end of the First World War many countries that were under the control of powerful empires began to seek independence. The first nationalist challenge to take place was against the British Empire in 1916.

Ireland had been bound to English rule for 700 years and there had been many rebellions in that time. By 1914, Britain was ready to allow Ireland a little more independence, but the war changed all this. In the north of Ireland, in an area called Ulster, **Protestants** had been settled for centuries. They showed their loyalty to Britain by volunteering to fight in the war. Almost as many Irishmen outside of Ulster also joined the British army. There were a large group of nationalists, however, who wanted complete independence for Ireland, and they refused to fight for Britain. They wanted to break free from the British Empire and set up an Irish republic.

The Easter Rising

On Easter Monday, April 1916, armed Irish nationalists took over the General Post Office in Dublin and declared their country was an Irish Republic. Other nationalists took up military positions around the city and the event came to be known as the Easter Rising. Powerful British troops put down the rebellion, arrested 3,500 nationalists, and put 170 on trial for **treason**. Of the people arrested, sixteen were executed.

The US Navy

When the United States joined the war in 1917, the country had no air force and a very small army. The US Navy, though, was the second largest in the world. It provided protection for the ships carrying troops and supplies to Europe. Building work on new ships began and **conscription** was introduced to increase the size of the army. By August 1918, three months before the end of the war, there were 1.5 million US soldiers in Europe.

Soldiers survey the wrecked interior of the General Post Office, Dublin, during the Easter Rising of 1916.

At first, there was little support in Ireland for the Easter Rising. This changed after the executions, and nationalist feelings grew stronger than ever before. By 1919, the nationalists had set up an Irish Republican Army (IRA). They prepared to fight Britain and launched a bitter guerrilla war.

Other British colonies heard about what was happening in Ireland. This strengthened nationalist feelings and the desire for independence in these countries also.

Revolution in Russia

Tsar Nicholas II's decision to lead Russia into the First World War proved to be a disastrous one. Battles were lost fighting German and Austro-Hungarian armies. Soldiers morale was low and by February 1917 there were strikes and demonstrations in Petrograd. This time, unlike what happened in 1905, the majority of the army refused to fire on the demonstrators. The Tsar had lost his authority and had no choice but to **abdicate** and hand over power to a new government.

The Bolsheviks and Lenin

The new government kept Russia in the war but soldiers were protesting and disobeying orders. In cities **revolutionaries** were setting up councils, called Soviets, for workers and soldiers. They were calling for an end to the war and radical changes to society. There were severe shortages of food and wages were falling. In the countryside, **peasants** began seizing the land of large private estates.

One group of revolutionaries was called the Bolsheviks. They wanted an immediate end to the war and for large country estates to be divided up and given to peasants. Their slogan was "peace, bread, and land". People began to believe that only the Bolsheviks could save the country from the war and economic chaos.

Vladimir Ilyich Lenin was a leading Bolshevik, but he had been forced to leave Russia after the 1905 revolution. In April 1917, the German army were happy to transport him back to Petrograd because they knew he was against the war. Once back in Russia, Lenin began organizing the Bolsheviks towards taking power from the government.

Lenin

Vladimir Ilyich Lenin became a revolutionary in 1893 at the age of 23. In 1895, he was imprisoned for opposing the Tsar and sent to Siberia in northern Russia until 1900. After that he lived in western Europe as well as spending time back in Russia. Lenin argued that workers needed a strong group of revolutionaries to help them overthrow the government and create a communist country. After the revolution in February 1917, Lenin became the leading Bolshevik. After the October revolution he became the leader of the new Russian government.

Vladimir Ilyich Lenin, the leader of the Bolsheviks, addresses a huge crowd in Petrograd (now known as St Petersburg) in Russia, 1 March 1917.

Revolution

In September 1917, the general in charge of the Russian army attempted to transport troops by train to Petrograd to put down the Bolsheviks. His trains were stopped by workers, many of whom were Bolsheviks, and the Russian army soldiers were persuaded to disobey their orders. The following month, in a carefully planned and mostly peaceful revolution, the Bolsheviks took power and replaced the government that had been formed in February.

In March 1918 Leon Trotsky, another leading Bolshevik, signed peace terms with Germany and ended Russia's involvement in the First World War.

Genocide and civil war

Turkey lost its influence in the Balkans in 1913 and blamed Serb nationalism for this. When Austria-Hungary declared war against Serbia in 1914, Turkey supported Austria-Hungary and joined the fighting.

The Armenian genocide

The Armenian population of eastern Turkey wanted independence. They had their own language, culture, and religion. Most did not join Turkey in the First World War and Turkey accused them of being disloyal. Turkey then went on to blame Armenians for all of its problems. The government decided to get rid of them.

In 1915, Armenian men in the Turkish army were forced to give up their arms. They were put into labour camps and either worked to death or executed. In towns and villages all over eastern Turkey, Armenian men were gathered together and marched away from their families before being killed. Women and children were driven out of their homes and forced into the desert of the neighbouring country, Syria, where they were left to die. Many died of starvation along the way or were beaten to death on the journey. It is estimated that over 1 million Armenians died in the **genocide** of 1915–1916.

The bodies of Armenian children, who were massacred in Turkey in 1915, lie side-by-side in a mass grave.

Russia invaded

In January 1918, a civil war broke out in Russia as anti-Bolshevik forces fought against Lenin's Bolshevik government. Forces opposing the Bolsheviks and their Red Army (the "Reds") became known as the "Whites" and they wanted to restore the old Russian empire. They were joined by foreign troops – British, French, US, and Japanese – who were sent to help defeat the Bolsheviks and bring Russia back into the First World War. Western governments also wanted to defeat the Bolsheviks because there was a danger that their **communist** ideas would spread across Europe.

Large parts of the old Russian empire were invaded and held by the Whites. By 1919, they were advancing towards Moscow, where the Reds held power, from all directions. The Reds came close to being defeated, but in 1921 they achieved victory and the civil war came to an end.

Members of the Bolshevik Red Army carry banners bearing mottos of support for Lenin's government, during the civil war of 1918.

The end of the Romanovs

The Romanov family had ruled Russia from 1613 until the Russian revolution in February 1917. After Tsar Nicholas II abdicated the plan was that he and his family would leave the country, but Bolshevik revolutionaries stopped them from going. They were kept under arrest, but the Bolsheviks were worried that the Whites would try to rescue the family. They decided to kill all of them. On the night of 16 July 1918 they were taken down to the cellar of the house where they were being held, and shot. Since that time there were always rumours that some of them were not killed and in 1992 the remains of the family were dug up for scientific tests. When the results were published in 1994, they claimed to prove that the remains were those of all of the Romanovs. However many people are still not convinced, and the case is by no means closed!

The Treaty of Versailles

Beginning in January 1919, at the palace of Versailles outside Paris, France, the victorious nations of the First World War met to draw up a peace settlement. Britain, France, and the United States decided upon the terms of the Treaty of Versailles.

Wilson's "Fourteen Points"

US President Woodrow Wilson saw himself as a referee between the warring nations, and in 1918 he drew up a famous list of "fourteen points". These set out how the countries should behave towards each other. They included:
- the right of countries to **govern** themselves
- the reduction of arms and weapons in every country
- the setting up of a **League of Nations** to help settle future conflicts.

However, Wilson could not persuade the **US Congress** to join the new League of Nations and the United States remained outside, while all the other countries joined.

New states

It was difficult for some countries in eastern Europe to set up their own governments because some **ethnic groups** were spread across different countries. Germans in Austria were not allowed to join with their fellow Germans, and other Germans found themselves living in part of the new country of Czechoslovakia, which was created out of the old Austro-Hungarian empire. Poland became a country once more, out of land that had been part of the old Russian empire and part of Germany.

The new borders of Europe after the agreement of the Treaty of Versailles.

Areas lost by Germany
Demilitarized zone
Areas lost by Russia
Areas lost by Austro-Hungarian Empire

Punishing Germany

Germany was not allowed any say in the terms of the Treaty of Versailles. Instead, the country was forced to take the blame for the First World War. The German ports were still being blockaded, which meant that food supplies were not getting into the country and people were starving. The country had no choice but to accept punishment. Germany lost land, which meant over 6 million Germans now lived in other countries and nearly 15 per cent of Germany's economic resources were lost. Germany also had to give up its colonies and a lot of its merchant ships. The German navy was reduced to only a few ships and the army's aircraft and weapons were taken away. As if that was not enough, Germany had to pay huge fines to the Allies called reparations.

Defeated German troops march home in silence, 14 December 1918.

Germans were left with the feeling that they were being unfairly punished for a war that they had not started alone. This created a strong feeling of resentment, which, in the 1930s, the new leader of Germany, Adolf Hitler, would promise to put right.

Taking the blame

Article 231 of the Treaty of Versailles –known as the "war guilt clause":

"…Germany accepts the responsibility of Germany and her allies for causing all the loss and damage which the Allies have suffered as a consequence of the war imposed upon them by the aggression of Germany and her allies."

(FROM *INTERNATIONAL HISTORY OF THE TWENTIETH CENTURY* BY BEST, HANHIMÄKI, MAIOLO, AND SCHULZE)

Many people across the world were angered and saddened by the terrible fighting that was happening during the First World War. Some people began to question the reasons for the war. As the war dragged on and the death toll continued to rise, these feelings began to creep into general society. After the war was over, life did not simply go back to normal. Society had changed dramatically.

Dadaism

During the war many artists went to the city of Zurich because Switzerland remained a **neutral** country that did not take part in the war. In the cafes of Zurich they talked, exchanged ideas, and thought about the kind of world that had created a war like this. An art movement known as Dadaism started there in 1916. The basis of it was disgust and anger at what was happening. Many of the artists were anarchists and they blamed governments, and people who supported governments, for the horrors of the war.

George Grosz's painting, *Republican Automatons*, shows how Germans supported their government, despite the horrors of the First World War.

Dadaism was against all war and it blamed European societies for allowing the war to take place. Dadaists made fun of anything that society took seriously. At the Cabaret Voltaire cafe in Zurich they organized various performances of song, music, and poetry that made fun of traditional art. Hugo Ball's poem "Karawane" was deliberately meaningless – it began, "Zimzim urallala zimzim Zanzibar…" – and it was chanted along with wild sounds that made it even more meaningless! Dadaists were trying to make the point that art was useless because it had failed to stop the war.

Dadaism spreads

Towards the end of the war, some Dada artists settled in Germany and their ideas became more influential. German Dadaists such as George Grosz and Otto Dix painted figures and faces deformed by war wounds that were deliberately shocking. The art movement also developed in New York, United States, where the French artist Marcel Duchamp shocked the art world by exhibiting everyday objects, like a toilet bowl, as if they were fine art.

This is a typical Dadaist painting by Otto Dix, called *German War Wounded Playing Cards* (1920).

Ernest Hemingway

Ernest Hemingway was born in Illinois, United States, and became a reporter for the *Kansas City Star* newspaper after graduating from high school. He was an ambulance driver for the American Red Cross in the First World War and was injured a few months before the end of the war. He went on to become a famous novelist and short-story writer, and was awarded the Nobel Prize for Literature in 1954.

One of Hemingway's most famous books, *A Farewell to Arms*, is about an American in the Italian ambulance service during the First World War. The story is set against feelings of great sadness and loss as a result of the war.

The end of an era

After the war there was a general feeling that European civilization had let itself down. This was summed up by a film made in 1919 by Abel Gance, called *J-accuse* (I accuse). In the film, dead soldiers rise from a battlefield cemetery – bandaged from war wounds and walking on crutches – and return to their villages to see if they had given their lives for something worthwhile. Shocked by their arrival, the villagers change their ways and live a better life.

A convoy of horses and wagons pass through the ruins of St. Martin's Church in Ypres, Belgium – just one of the many villages and cities virtually destroyed during the First World War.

European progress?

Throughout the 19th century and into the early years of the 20th, Europe had set itself up as a standard for the rest of the world to follow. The empires of Britain, France, and Germany claimed to be bringing progress and civilization to all parts of the world.

Many people thought, however, that the horrors of the First World War had shown European culture as **barbaric**. The war seemed to have achieved nothing of value and countries had tumbled into it blindly. The 1917 revolution in Russia promised a better country, built on co-operation rather than competition, and in the years to come many countries would turn to communism for this reason. Elsewhere, a better world was promised by those who wanted a return to the traditional values that the Dadaists mocked. Authority, strict order, and anti-communism would be held up as the answer to Europe's decline. In Germany (the country that was blamed for causing the First World War) this would give rise to Adolf Hitler and the Nazi Party.

American isolationism

In 1919, when President Wilson returned home after the meeting at Versailles, a Republican Party hoping to win power in the 1920 elections opposed him. Wilson went on a speaking tour of the United States, hoping to win people over to his side, but it was too much of a strain and he collapsed in Colorado in September 1919. He suffered a stroke in October and died on 3 February 1924.

Republican Warren G. Harding became president in 1921 and the international way of thinking that Wilson stood for was abandoned. The affairs of Europe were not seen as important to the US economy. The United States could become a world power on its own without the help of an old Europe that had torn itself apart in war.

For ordinary people everywhere, between the time of the Wright Brothers and that of the Treaty of Versailles, the world had changed enormously and it would never be the same again.

Fearful of the future

By 1919, many people in power were worried that the old order was being questioned.

David Lloyd George, Britain's Prime Minister wrote, "The whole of Europe is filled with the spirit of revolution. The existing order, in it's political, social, and economic aspects, is questioned by the mass of the population from one end of Europe to the other."

Edward M. House, a United States representative at Versailles, wrote in his diary, "[Communism] is gaining ground everywhere. We are sitting upon an open [gun] powder **magazine** and some day a spirit may ignite it."

(FROM A PEOPLE'S HISTORY OF THE WORLD BY CHRIS HANMAN.)

TIMELINE

1900

Boxer rebellion in China
Britain raises the starting age for
    miners from twelve to thirteen
The Labour Party formed in the UK
An airship reaches a height of
    305 metres (1,000 feet)
World's first automatic telephone
    exchange becomes operational
Freud's *The Interpretation of Dreams*
    is published
Picasso leaves Spain and travels to
    Paris by train

1901

Queen Victoria dies on 22 January
President McKinley assassinated on
    14 September
Commonwealth of Australia formed
US troops crush rebellion in the
    Philippines
Marconi makes the first wireless
    transmission across the
    Atlantic Ocean
The Gillette safety razor goes on sale
First electric vacuum cleaner
    invented
Over 100,000 spectators watch the
    Football Association (FA) Cup
    Final at Crystal Palace in London.

1902

Women achieve the right to vote
    in national elections in Australia
End of Boer War in southern Africa
Theodore Roosevelt goes on a
    hunting trip and refuses to shoot
    a helpless bear

1903

First powered flight by an aeroplane
Roger Casement makes public the ill
    treatment of Africans in the Congo
United States intervene in Panama

1904

Outbreak of the Russian-Japanese war
Rebellion by the Herero people
    in southern Africa
United States intervene in the
    Dominican Republic

1905

End of the Russian-Japanese war
The Industrial Workers of the
    World organization formed in
    the United States
Einstein publishes scientific papers,
    including the claim that $E=mc^2$
A group of modern artists,
    exhibiting their work in Paris,
    are described as "wild beasts"
    (*fauves*) by a critic
First purpose-built cinema opens,
    in Pittsburgh in the United States

1906

Strikes in France crushed by
    the army

1907

Picasso paints *Les Demoiselles
    D'Avignon*
First portable vacuum cleaner
    invented

1908

Bosnia forced to become part of the
Austro-Hungarian empire
Jack Johnson becomes the first black
boxing champion

1909

Spanish troops refuse an order to
fire on strikers

1911

Striking dock workers shot dead by
troops in England

1912

United States intervenes in
Nicaragua

1912–13

War in the Balkans and the expulsion
of Ottoman forces from the region

1913

A suffragette grabs the reins of
a horse during the Derby horse
race and dies
Modern European art exhibited at
the Armory Show in New York

1914

Outbreak of First World War

1915

British, Australian, and New
Zealand troops land on Gallipoli
The *Lusitania* sunk in the Atlantic

1915–1916

The Armenian genocide

1916

Battles of Verdun and Somme
Easter Rising in Dublin, Ireland
Dadaism emerges in Zurich
Emma Goldman imprisoned in the
United States for distributing
literature on birth control

1917

Revolution in Russia in February and
again in October
The US enters the First World War
Battle of Passchendaele

1918

End of First World War
British, French, American, and
Japanese troops invade Russia
Execution of the Tsar and his family
Women achieve the right to vote
in national elections in Britain
Woodrow Wilson issues his
"fourteen points" as a model for
future relations between countries

1919

The victorious nations meet to draw
up a peace settlement at Versailles
Woodrow Wilson suffers a stroke
and later dies in 1924
John Maynard Keynes writes *The
Economic Consequences of Peace*
Abel Gance makes the film *J-accuse*

FURTHER INFORMATION

CDs

Eyewitness: The 1900s (BBC Audiobooks, 2004)
Eyewitness: The 1910s (BBC Audiobooks, 2004)

Books

Armies of the Past: Going to War in World War I, Adrian Gilbert (Franklin Watts, 2001)
Artists in Profile: Cubists, Jeremy Wallis (Heinemann Library, 2002)
Disaster! Titanic: The Tragedy at Sea, Kathleen W. Deady (Capstone Press, 2002)
Lenin and the Russian Revolution in World History, Ann Malaspina (Enslow, 2000)
20th Century Art: 1900–10: New Ways of Seeing, Jackie Gaff (Heinemann Library, 2000)
20th Century Fashion: 1900–20: Linen and Lace, Sue Mee (Heinemann Library, 1999)
20th Century Media: 1900–20: Sound & Light, Steve Parker (Heinemann Library, 2002)
20th Century Music: 1900–20: New Horizons, Malcolm Hayes (Heinemann Library, 2001)
20th Century Perspectives: The Causes of World War I, Tony Allan (Heinemann Library, 2002)
20th Century Science & Technology: 1900–20 Shrinking World, Steve Parker (Heinemann Library, 2000)

Websites

http://en.wikipedia.org/wiki/1900s
This encyclopedia has sections on the 1900s and the 1910s.

http://elegantmusings.com/links.html
Online historical fashion collections and a study on cinematic costume.

http://www.scholiast.org/history/timetables/
History timelines for all eras – take a look at 1900–1919.

Disclaimer

All the internet addresses (URLs) given in this book were valid at the time of going to press. However, due to the dynamic nature of the Internet, some addresses may have changed, or sites may have ceased to exist since publication. While the author and publishers regret any inconvenience this may cause readers, no responsibility for any such changes can be accepted by either the author or the publishers.

the early 1900s to 1919

Books and literature	• *The Wonderful Wizard of Oz* by L. Frank Baum (1900) • *The Hound of the Baskervilles* by Arthur Conan Doyle (1902) • *Pollyanna* by Eleanor H. Porter (1913)
Education	• Annual teachers pay in the United States is US$325 • The first elementary school in the United States is founded by John Dewey
Fads and fashions	• Ping Pong is invented in the UK • The Sunday drive becomes a national pastime • Teddy Bears are mass produced in the United States from 1905
Historic events	• Different types of blood in the human body are discovered • In the United States, the world's first book of stamps is issued • British ex-army officer Robert Baden-Powell founds the Boy Scout youth movement
Music, film, and theatre	• Scott Joplin makes ragtime music popular • The United States National Board of Censorship is formed to make guidelines for censoring films
People	• SS Chief Heinrich Himmler is born in 1900 • Irish-born poet Oscar Wilde dies • Jeanette Rankin becomes the first woman elected to US Congress

GLOSSARY

abdicate to give up a position and its title, usually one of power

allies the countries at war against Germany, Austria-Hungary, Turkey, and Bulgaria in the First World War

ambassador someone who represents someone else or another country

anarchist someone who believes society can be organized without the need for any form of control

arms race fight between two countries to have more powerful weapons

artillery medium-to-heavy guns used by an army

assassinate to deliberately target and kill someone

assembly line way in which a factory produces its goods in as fast a time as possible

atom building block of all matter

atomic bomb weapon of mass destruction, releasing an atom's energy

barbaric uncivilized, with total disregard for other people's rights

birth control preventing pregnancy

blockade methods used to prevent something happening

colony country ruled over by another country as part of an empire

communist person who believes in government ownership and spreading wealth

concentration camp prison camp where people are forced to live

conscious fully aware of, not hidden

conscription compulsory call-up for military service

culture ways in which a society or a group expresses itself

deadlock unable to reach agreement

Democrat member of the Democrats, a political party in the United States

discrimination making a choice on the basis of, for example, race or religion

dominant in a position of power over other people or groups

economy matters to do with money

electron part of the make-up of every atom

empire control of other countries by a dominant power

era period of time with a character of its own

ethnic group group with a common nationality or a common culture

genocide deliberate and organized killing of a group of people with the intention of destroying their identity as an ethnic, cultural, or religious group

ghetto very poor neighbourhood

govern rule over

guerrilla form of fighting against larger and more powerful forces which avoids an open battle

heir someone in a position to inherit something

hunger strike refusing to take food or water as a form of protest

immigrant person who travels to another country to live there

industrialization the period of change from a society based on agriculture to one based on modern industry and factory production

inferior of less worth than something else

League of Nations international organization, resembling the United Nations, set up after the First World War to peacefully settle arguments between nations

magazine chamber for a supply of bullets inside a gun

mass production when something is made in factories by machines in large numbers rather than one at a time by an individual

migrant someone who travels, often from one country to another, in order to find work

mobilize prepare for active service

mutiny open rebellion against authority

nationalist person with a strong belief in the value of the nation to which they belong

neutral not belonging to any side in a dispute or argument

parliament place where politicians make decisions and pass laws

patriotism when someone strongly identifies with their country

peasant poor person who works on the land

peninsula narrow strip of land surrounded mostly by water

pension fixed and regular payment due after a period of work

Protestant set of Christian beliefs belonging to the Protestant church

psychological to do with the mind

radical getting to the roots of a problem by suggesting deep-seated changes

rebellion rising up against an authority

republic form of government without a king or queen

revolutionaries people planning to overthrow a government

socialism belief that life would be better if organized around the needs of people rather than the making of money and profits

social security government system of payments designed to help the poor

strike refusing to work in order to obtain better pay or working conditions

suffragette women who campaigned for the right to vote

suspicion not trusting someone else

territory land belonging to someone

trade union organization formed by workers to protect their interests

transmission information communicated by one group to another

treason acting in a way that helps the enemy of your country

trench ditch dug in the ground, around 2 metres (7 feet) deep, which housed soldiers during battles

unconscious not fully aware of something but existing in the background

US Congress the law-making body of the United States

INDEX

Titles in the *Modern Eras Uncovered* series include:

Hardback   1 844 43950 X

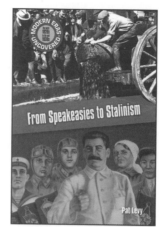

Hardback   1 844 43951 8

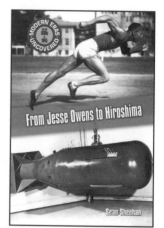

Hardback   1 844 43952 6

Hardback   1 844 43953 4

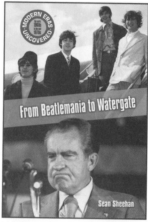

Hardback   1 844 43955 0

Hardback   1 844 43956 9

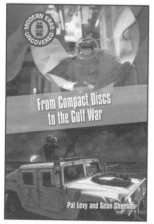

Hardback   1 844 43957 7

Hardback   1 844 43958 5

Find out about the other titles in this series on our website www.raintreepublishers.co.uk